W9-CGR-411

Pleasant Dreams

Nighttime Meditations for Peace of Mind

Amy E. Dean

Hay House, Inc.
Carlsbad, California • Sydney, Australia

Copyright © 2000 by Amy E. Dean

Published and distributed in the United States by:
Hay House, Inc., P.O. Box 5100, Carlsbad, CA 92018-5100
(800) 654-5126 • (800) 650-5115 (fax)

Editorial: Jill Kramer • *Cover Design:* Christy Salinas • *Interior Design:* Julie Davison
Illustrations: Julie Paschkis

All rights reserved. No part of this book may be reproduced by any mechanical, photographic, or electronic process, or in the form of a phonographic recording; nor may it be stored in a retrieval system, transmitted, or otherwise be copied for public or private use—other than for "fair use" as brief quotations embodied in articles and reviews without prior written permission of the publisher.

The intent of the author is only to offer information of a general nature to help you in your quest for emotional and spiritual well-being. In the event you use any of the information in this book for yourself, which is your constitutional right, the author and the publisher assume no responsibility for your actions.

Library of Congress Cataloging-in-Publication Data

Dean, Amy.
    Pleasant dreams : nighttime meditations for peace of mind / Amy E. Dean.
        p. cm.
    ISBN 1-56170-693-0
        1. Affirmations. 2. Peace of mind. I. Title.

BF697.5.S47 D426 2000
158.1'28—dc21

                                                    99-057405

[Material based on *Pleasant Dreams* © 1993 by Amy E. Dean]

ISBN 1-56170-693-0

03 02 01 00   4 3 2 1
1st printing, October 2000

Printed in China by Imago

Introduction

"Now I lay me down to sleep" is the beginning of a comforting childhood prayer that you may have recited when you were young. Thinking back to those nights so long ago, you may remember times when a parent read you your favorite bedtime story or tucked you into bed each night. A soft kiss on your cheek was a reminder of love; the soft glow of a night-light or a door positioned to stay slightly ajar provided reassurance that you were safe and snug in the darkness. As you lay in your soft, warm bed—perhaps with your favorite doll or stuffed animal nestled in your arms—the promise of a new day helped you journey into the world of pleasant dreams.

But for adults, such peaceful pre-sleep preparations rarely occur. And, too often, stress and worry make it hard to enjoy the benefits of a restful, relaxing, and revitalizing night's sleep. While each dawn may still hold the promise of a new beginning, drifting easily off into slumber and staying asleep throughout the night may seem to be benefits reserved solely for the very young.

Pleasant Dreams will help restore your inner peace when darkness falls so you can make your journey into the night calmly and peacefully, ready to let go of the hustle and bustle of daily life. Each meditation is intended to be a nighttime cup of warm milk—to be savored in a soothing and relaxing manner so that you can enjoy pleasant dreams each week of the year.

May this book help you view your nights as eloquent endings to your days, as well as joyful beginnings to your tomorrows—and may it always help you find true peace of mind.

— Amy E. Dean

Tonight I feel like a complete,
whole, relaxed human being.
I think pleasant thoughts or do
something that brings me peace
and contentment.

Many people have things in their life that calm them, center them, or bring them inner peace. For some it is the ocean, with its smells, sounds, rhythm, and vastness. For others it is a spectacular sunset, where luminous colors spark each surrounding cloud into an ethereal hue. Still others may play a song that comforts them in some way.

What is it that brings *you* inner peace? Maybe running in the morning, downhill skiing at night, or watching dancing snowflakes in a gentle snowfall can make you feel good inside. These are your positive relaxation "fixes." When you haven't been skiing for a while, for instance, just running your hands down your skis or closing your eyes and remembering your last time flying down a snow-covered mountain can be as reassuring and soothing as the act of skiing itself.

When you do something that brings you inner peace, or you can close your eyes and recall a joyous memory, you can return to a state of happiness. Tonight, enjoy the reality of one of your positive relaxation fixes, or create it clearly in your mind—hear it, touch it, and experience it.

Tonight I keep in mind
that in order to be
completely balanced,
I need good food,
positive thoughts, and
loving relationships.

Whenever you feel out of sorts, find it hard to concentrate at the end of the day, or cannot sleep at night, you may struggle unsuccessfully to restore your inner balance. However, your problems may be related to three areas in your life where you may need to make changes. To find out, ask yourself these questions: "Am I eating right? Am I allowing time for meditation? Do I feel safe in my world?"

First, look at the foods you eat. Is your diet rich in nutrients provided by fresh fruits and vegetables, lean meat and fish, and whole grains? Are you drinking plenty of water throughout the day? Are you chewing your food slowly, or eating at a time or place where you don't feel rushed?

Next, consider how much time you set aside during the day to still your mind. Ideally, it's best to provide at least a half hour for communing with yourself and your Higher Power. Doing so prevents you from focusing on the treadmill of the daily grind, always worrying about the things you've yet to do.

Finally, roommate hassles, family pressures, and work stresses can contribute to the disruption of your inner peace. So, keep your home a haven, your relationships stable, and your work space comfortable. Paying attention to your diet, your quiet times, and your living and working conditions can work wonders for restoring balance to your body, mind, and soul.

Each night is a new beginning.
I take advantage of this time
to engage in new activities
with friends, family, or
new acquaintances.

Just as each day is a new beginning, so, too, can each evening be a new start. The darkness of a cold winter night doesn't limit you to hibernation; rather, it can present you with a multitude of exhilarating and energizing choices. After the sun has set, you can start on a project you've been putting off, such as taking an adult education class, joining a bowling league, or getting involved in a volunteering opportunity. It can be the time you take a courageous first step in getting to know someone new. It can also be the time to try a new recipe, read a good book, or take in a first-run movie.

Each night gives you the chance to recharge yourself after your day's batteries have run down. You are presented with endless opportunities to start anew on your goals, your growth, and your interests. Instead of using the time you've been given tonight reflecting on the past events of the day, you can enjoy each moment in the here and now.

Although the day is done, tomorrow has yet to come. There are plans you can make, places you can go, people you can see, and projects you can complete. Rest assured that tonight isn't just a closing; it's also an opening to greater things.

My day has been good,
and I've done well. Tonight
I'm feeling content and
satisfied and am ready to
let slumber overtake me.

This evening, your reward for everything you did during the day is a good night's sleep. To make your sleep more peaceful and relaxing and filled with pleasant thoughts, set aside a few minutes to gently close your mind on the day's events.

Before you turn off the lights, visualize walking down a pleasant, nature-filled path. Each step you take moves you further from the day's activities and the many tasks you undertook. Look around you as you walk. Breathe deeply. See lakes and mountains, and hear the soothing sounds of a babbling brook. Watch the rise and fall of gentle ocean waves that reflect a glorious sunset; breathe deeply of the humid air in a tropical rain forest while being serenaded by an orchestra of jungle sounds. In the inner sanctuary you create in your mind, nothing is important— nothing except peace of mind and the hours ahead in which your mind will be gently stilled.

As you reach the end of your nature walk, you may feel the tensions and pressures of the day fall from your shoulders. Your body may feel lighter. Your lips may be turned upwards to form a gentle smile. You may feel a yawn building in your chest. Now tell yourself, "Today has been good. I can close my eyes and let the reward of sleep drift over me."

Tonight I imagine the most
joyous situations and let
them become part of my
sleeping thoughts. After a
night of delightful dreams,
I wake up refreshed and ready
to continue thinking positively.

It has been said that if you tell yourself what you'd like to dream before you go to sleep, over time you can teach yourself to create your own dreams. If you've been troubled by restless nights or nightmares that disturb your sleep, beginning tonight you can reprogram your mind. How can you do this? One way is to train your mind to think positive thoughts. You can say, for example, "I release any dreams about my day at work. Instead, I'll dream about the fun activities I'll do this weekend" or "I let go of any confusing, stress-filled dreams. Instead, I'll dream about an island paradise."

Another way to reprogram your dreams is to ask that the answers to questions that are troubling you be revealed. Before going to sleep, for example, you can say, "I've been bothered lately by physical ailments. What can I do to improve my health?" or "What's the best way to handle my latest conflict with my boss?"

A final way to reprogram is to prepare yourself for a night of relaxing or revealing dreams by visualizing what you'd most like to dream about. Close your eyes and "see" yourself doing what you want to do or being who you want to be. Immediately after this visualization, go to sleep. A good night's sleep may actually help you finish the dream you already started.

Tonight I trust that the
natural rhythms of my life
will lead me to a calm and
peaceful night's sleep.
I wake up refreshed.

Everything in nature changes. You can trust that the sun and moon will rise and set, the tide will ebb and flow, and the seasons will change.

Because you can trust that such things will happen, you can also trust that they're part of a natural rhythm. So, you don't get up every morning and worry whether the sun will rise; you don't stand on a beach at low tide, concerned that the waves won't return to shore. Without your doing anything, nature takes care of itself.

So it is with people. Everyone laughs and cries. Everyone works and plays. Everyone is born, and everyone dies. Just as nature has its natural flow, so, too, do people.

There are also natural rhythms in your life: one that helps you awaken—the flow rhythm—and one that guides you to sleep—the ebb rhythm. Tonight your natural ebb rhythm—which is expressed by physical fatigue, mental exhaustion, and the desire for closure—can lead you to peace and relaxation. If you can go with that flow and trust it—just like you trust everything in nature—you'll experience calmness and the chance to revitalize yourself for tomorrow. Now is the time to follow your natural rhythms and sleep in peace.

A pile of sawdust that
gathers under woodworking
can never go back to its
previous form. To accept the
present, I must begin to work
with new pieces of wood and
make new piles of sawdust.

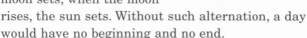

S unrise and sunset together represent the measure of a day. When the sun rises, the moon sets; when the moon rises, the sun sets. Without such alternation, a day would have no beginning and no end.

There are cycles in your life as well. There are endings as well as beginnings. A layoff from a job means the end of your employment with that particular company, but it also signals the beginning of a new job elsewhere. The termination of a long-term relationship means the end of your time with that particular person, but it also signals the beginning of your time spent with someone else. An illness or injury means the end of the way you've lived life up until that point, but it also signals the beginning of a new, healing way of living.

It's a sign of wisdom to be able to recognize such cycles of life when they occur, and to also accept them. Without such acceptance, your energy stays focused solely on what you've lost, and you remain stagnant. To live and grow, you must be in motion.

Tonight, remember that you can never go back to the past, nor will the past become the present— even if the past was only yesterday or just this morning. To live in the present, accept that everything you do from this moment on must be clean, fresh, and new.

15

Tonight, I clear my mind
of intrusive thoughts
and let my body and
mind completely relax.
I fall asleep easily.

Have you ever wondered why you're sometimes more awake at night than during the day? From the moment you arise in the morning until it's time to go to bed, you may feel as if you're trying to negotiate through a vast sea of thick pea soup. Your body may feel physically heavy while your mind seems lost in a fog.

But the moment your head hits the pillow, you may feel as if you're sailing free on a shining sea. Your body may feel energized, while your mind spills out thoughts and ideas like an active newswire machine. Perhaps you're excited about an upcoming trip or vacation. Maybe you're anticipating seeing old friends again. Perhaps you're in the process of house hunting or have just moved into a new home. Or maybe you're thinking about leaving your job and going off on your own to start a new business. After the burden of thinking about other people, places, and things is relieved at the end of the day and you've had a chance to wind down, it's understandable that all of these thoughts tumbling through your mind might keep you from falling asleep.

Tonight, instead of staying up all night thinking about what has been or what may be, try to completely clear your mind of any thoughts. Breathe deeply, relax your body from head to toe . . . and gently drift off to sleep.

To nurture my life energy,
I need to make time tonight
to withdraw from the hustle
and bustle of the world so
I can get a good night's rest.
Doing so can increase my
emotional, physical, and
spiritual strength.

When do you allow yourself time to rest? When you're sick? When your muscles are so sore that it hurts to move? When several sleepless nights catch up to you?

If you're like most people, you probably don't set aside time for rest until your body cries out for it. But by getting into the habit of listening to your body, you can "tune in" to the messages your body gives you that signal a need for rest. Tight muscles, a backache, a slight headache, stiff shoulders, tired eyes, and poor concentration are just a few rest-related messages.

Taking a rest doesn't mean doing nothing. It simply means slowing your pace, becoming less active, and easing some of your tension. Lying down for a few moments is resting; and so is going to a movie, reading a good book, watching television, listening to music, or talking to friends.

Rest allows the body time to release tension and return to a more normal, balanced state. And when you're well rested, you're often more energized. As the Chinese explain the lesson of the tortoise, which knows when to withdraw into itself and when to restore its energy: "The tortoise is good at nurturing energy, so it can survive a century without food."

I pay attention to the noises
that keep me up at night or
that awaken me from a sound
sleep. I take the necessary
measures to mitigate these
unpleasant sounds.

Nighttime noise in and around your home—coming from a television, from others who live with you, from planes flying overhead, or from automobile traffic—is a common source of sleep interruption. In fact, studies have shown that most people who live near airports or busy streets rarely adjust to the racket, leading to poor sleep.

Rather than letting a noisy environment impact your sleep, you can take steps to minimize the effects of the noise. If you live near an airport or busy thoroughfare, or room with others who are on a different sleep schedule than you are, deaden the noise by padding your floors in your bedroom with thick carpeting. Cover your windows with heavy drapes, or invest in soundproof windows. Block out unwanted sounds by wearing earplugs to bed or by playing a tape of soothing music. Or, drown out the intrusive sounds with a fan, an air conditioner, or a white-noise machine.

I create my own sense
of peace and contentment
by adjusting the situations
in my life that don't bring
me comfort. I nestle
comfortably in my
new nest of pleasure.

𝒜 bird builds its nest by searching for the perfect twigs, weeds, and pieces of string and paper. Then it patiently interweaves these materials until its nest achieves the right shape, size, depth, and warmth. Once completed, the bird stops its nest-building and spends its time nestled comfortably in its home.

To be at peace with yourself, you first need to construct your own nest. This nest could be an apartment, the home you've always dreamed of, or a quiet room. But your nest doesn't always have to be a place. Your nest can be created from intangible things that bring you peace: freedom from negative thinking or co-dependency, for example; a daily hug from a loved one; or time set aside for enjoyment and relaxation.

Without such comforting "nests" in your life, peace can be difficult to achieve. From now on, you can start to "build" your nest by attending a helpful support group, rearranging your schedule to set aside precious moments just for yourself, communicating to your partner the things he or she can do to make you feel comforted, or spending time with positive people doing enjoyable activities. Such things can help you create a comforting nest of pleasure.

I am as grateful for the
night as I am for the day.
This evening, I go for a short
"mental hike" and let the night
air soak into every pore,
cleansing and comforting me.

The natural beauty of the night can be spectacular. Sometimes there's a bright, full moon  that glows like an ethereal white disk against an ink-black sky, liberally sprinkled with sparkling stars. Perhaps you see this image reflected on the shimmering waters of a country lake. Or you may see it in a warm rain puddle on the side of a city street as you marvel at the magical kingdom of colors created by the twinkling city lights.

If you can use your senses to the fullest, there's so much beauty you can find during the night. Open your eyes to the silhouettes of the trees and buildings around you and the shadows that dance in the glow of streetlights. Listen to bullfrogs croaking, crickets chirping, or the wind howling. Breathe deeply of the cool, clean air, and take in the aromas of spring growth. Imagine the feeling of the evening on your face as it gently caresses you. Open your mouth, and mentally taste the delicate flavors of countless raindrops.

Tonight, take a "mental" walk through peaceful, natural surroundings. Appreciate the sensual beauty of the evening by using all of your senses. Let the night touch you in a way that brings you contentment and enjoyment. Then, let everything you've seen, smelled, heard, touched, and tasted lull you into a soothing sleep.

As I "write" the ending to my
story tonight, I tie up all the
loose ends from the beginning
and middle so I can close
the "book" on today with
a satisfied, contented sigh.

Every good story has a beginning, a middle, and an end. The beginning is like your morning, full of newness, promise, and hope. This morning was your introduction to a new day—a chance to meet new people and have new experiences.

The middle of the story is how your day progressed. It includes all the actions and events, the dialogues and the locales, and the conflicts and confrontations you experienced. The middle may have been dull and boring or it could have raced along at a fast pace. But no matter how it unfolded, you may have gotten to know the characters in your story a little better or learned a little more about yourself.

The ending of the story is this evening. Although not all of it has been written, you may have already found resolutions to the conflicts and compromises in the middle of the story, as well as logical endings to some of the events that started at the beginning.

Now you need to write the story's conclusion. You can add more conflict, confrontation, and dramas; or you can end with a feeling of hope, gratitude, and peace. How will you complete your story— with a finale that demands a sequel, or with a happy ending?

From this moment on, I set aside my tensions from today and my worries about tomorrow. When I can relax during my time away from work and obligations, I am much happier.

After a hectic day, how easy is it for you to switch gears and relax? Because your free time is often in short supply, it may be hard to slow down your pace, not feel frantic and tense, and enjoy simple pleasures.

There are many things you can do to make a swift and effective transition from work time to leisure time. Begin by "de-stressing" while traveling home at the end of the day. Listen to soothing music in the car, or use progressive muscle relaxation— alternately tense and relax your muscles from head to toe as you breathe deeply—or read a novel or your favorite magazine on the bus or train.

Before you begin your evening, make a list of all the things you feel you have to accomplish the next day. Then tell yourself that there's nothing you can do about them now, so you won't use valuable time in the present dwelling on them.

Finally, do something on a regular basis that signifies that your busy day is over. Change into comfortable clothes, brew a cup of your favorite decaffeinated beverage, exercise, or take a hot bath. The particular "ritual" you do isn't as important as choosing an activity that becomes a "cue" that will help you relax and unwind at the end of the day.

Tonight I feel how
the rhythms of my body
interact with the natural
rhythms around me.
I know that I am
one with nature.

WEEK 15

Recognizing your oneness with the natural world can expand your horizons, give you a deeper sense of self, and help you move below the brittle surface of life to experience the soft undersides of nature.

There are many ways to "go out into nature." Physically, you can camp, hike, birdwatch, or work in your garden. Sensually, you can smell the richness of the soil, feel the rigid spine of a discarded bird feather, see the droplets of moisture on leaves, hear the songbirds bidding adieu to the day, and taste the first fresh herbs of the season. Spiritually, you can get closer to living, growing things.

Right now, take a deep breath and feel your connection with the natural wonders around you. Appreciate the harmony that nature has with the world and the process of growth in all living things. Feel how the natural world readies itself for a good night's sleep. Then tuck yourself comfortably in for the night in the same way. Say, "I am one with nature. I honor its growth and its vitality, as I honor mine. I respect it, as I respect myself. Each day I learn more about it, as I learn more about myself. And so my life is peaceful and harmonious with nature."

Just as a city dweller
can create an indoor garden
to grow fresh fruits and
vegetables, so too can I create
a "growing garden" out of any
one of my dreams. All I need
is time, determination, and a
willingness to make it happen.

Have you ever dreamed of owning the perfect home or winning wonderful awards? In 1970, when Peter Chan moved his family to their new home in Oregon, others who had seen his property couldn't understand why Chan had spent money on a yard filled with hard clay soil and large stones. But Chan didn't see his property as a problem. He saw it as an opportunity to fulfill a dream by creating a breathtaking garden. Today, his beautiful gardens have won awards and have been featured in magazines and on national television.

How did he use real life to interpret his dream? He enriched the clay soil with compost and used the stones that were viewed as "troublesome" to form pleasant pathways between the raised beds of his vegetable garden.

You may have dreams of your own—some more ambitious than Chan's, others equally so, and a few that are rather simple and easy to achieve. But there's much to learn from Chan's philosophy, which echoes that of many Chinese gardeners: *Use what you have wisely.*

Tonight, think about a dream you have. Consider the resources you'll need to achieve it. Then ask, "What do I have in my own life right now—materially and creatively—that can help make this dream a reality?"

I engage in stress-free
activities early in the evening
so that when I do lay myself
down to sleep, I do so quickly
and with ease. I wake up
feeling refreshed.

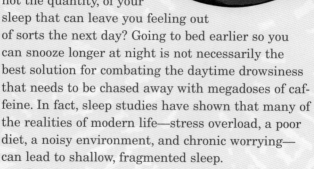

Do you know that it's often the quality, not the quantity, of your sleep that can leave you feeling out of sorts the next day? Going to bed earlier so you can snooze longer at night is not necessarily the best solution for combating the daytime drowsiness that needs to be chased away with megadoses of caffeine. In fact, sleep studies have shown that many of the realities of modern life—stress overload, a poor diet, a noisy environment, and chronic worrying—can lead to shallow, fragmented sleep.

But there are ways to "turn off" daytime thinking so you can "turn on" better sleep at night. First, complete your work, school, or family obligations at least two or three hours before going to bed. Use the "free time" for stress-free thinking—read a book, play a game, talk on the telephone with a friend, write a personal letter—or for thought-calming activities—meditate, take a hot bath, engage in a hobby, or watch a favorite movie or television show.

If you find that you still can't turn your mind off and continue to toss and turn in bed, go to another room and write down whatever is on your mind. Then engage in a quiet, calming activity until you finally feel drowsy.

I begin my prayers tonight
with "Now I lay me down
to sleep. I pray to my
Higher Power my soul to keep..."
Then I give my heartfelt
thanks for the day.

Some people believe that prayer is something that needs to be scheduled—a once-in-the-morning or a once-at-night routine. Yet, do you know that prayer isn't so much a ritual or a necessity as it is a conversation with a Higher Power—open, honest communication with a trusted spiritual partner? That means that you can pray any time and as often as you'd like.

Prayer in the morning can be a wonderful way to begin the day, but oftentimes your life can get so busy when you wake up that your prayers are like your breakfasts—unsatisfying, incomplete, and grabbed on the run. So, morning prayers may become just one more thing you try to fit into your life—something to do while shaving or showering or when you're driving to work on the freeway.

That's why it's important to keep in mind that tonight the door is open to your prayers. Your Higher Power is still there to listen to you. You can share your feelings of the day as if you were speaking to a close friend. All you have to do is start talking.

Then you can close the door on this day with prayer, knowing that you're carrying the good, warm feelings that faith can bring. When you finally lay down to sleep tonight, you can say good night to your Higher Power and rest in peace.

I'm ready to relax into a peaceful,
restful sleep. Tonight I loosen
the day's tension from my body
as well as my mind.

Your physical and mental states at bedtime are important. If you're tense, edgy, or feel a sense of failure and defeat as a result of the day's efforts, your sleep will probably be restless and unsatisfying. Instead of mentally winding down from the day or feeling physically at peace when you close your eyes, you may still feel that there are things you ought to do.

But what difference does it make if a few things are left undone? Will they matter ten years from now? Nothing is ever so important that it has to be accomplished right now. Nothing is ever so critical that your whole world will come crashing down if it's not immediately attended to.

Tonight, put the day to rest. Take a deep breath, then slowly release the air as you relax your shoulders. Breathe in again as you squeeze your hands into tight fists, then release your breath and open your hands. Feel the difference in your shoulders and hands now that you've released the tension of the day. Do the same with your mind. Take in a deep breath, then release all the chatter in your head.

We are all candle-lighters for each other. I know that I am never in the dark; I always have the ability to gather light and give it to others.

Are there people in your life who need your reassurance at night to help them sleep better? Maybe your children need you to tell them a story or tuck them in at night. Perhaps a family member who lives alone needs your nightly telephone call to feel safe and secure. Maybe a friend who's bedridden or going through a difficult time could use some of your concern and attention at night. Or perhaps new members of a 12-step support group would benefit from your message of strength and hope in order to guide them through another night of sobriety.

If you've ever seen a candlelight ceremony, you know how powerful just one candle can be. Countless tapers can be lit from that one small flame until a room, a large meeting hall—even a darkened avenue—is brilliant with light.

Sometimes others may see you as a small flame from which they can light their candles of hope, health, and happiness. So, each night, give the gift of your light to others. Offer encouragement to those who could use it, give support to those who are in need, provide strength to those who are weak or who are losing faith, and share your experience and knowledge with those who will listen. Don't leave anyone in the dark. Let others light their candles from yours.

Tonight I envision a peaceful,
calm world where the only
thing that matters is a good
night's sleep. My mind
relaxes and fills up with
the gentle sound of my
own breathing.

your reward for today's activities will be sleep. Although your body and mind may crave this slumber, it may  take some time to "turn off" stressful thoughts so you can relax your body.

To release energy from your body and fill your mind with pleasant thoughts, set aside some time before going to bed for a sleep-inducing meditation. Sit or lie down in a comfortable position, and close your eyes. In your mind, picture yourself walking down thickly carpeted stairs as you count slowly backwards from ten. With each step, imagine that you're descending closer to a lush forest glen. When you reach the last step, look around you. Perhaps you see a sparkling stream that reflects a shimmering full moon. Maybe there are distant mountains capped by a night sky decorated with twinkling stars. Perhaps the gentle hoot of an owl, the low "grumps" of bullfrogs, and the tender sounds of crickets fill the night air.

Now shift your attention to your breathing. As you inhale, imagine clear, fresh air going into your lungs. Bring the air slowly and deeply into your abdomen. Then release the air in a slow, steady exhalation, feeling your abdomen sink. Imagine your breath as a gentle breeze that barely stirs the leaves on the forest trees. Breathe in, breathe out. Fall asleep.

I give thanks for this day.
I praise the miracles that
are already on their way
for tomorrow. I express my
gratitude for the precious
gift of tonight.

Many people believe that the quality of each day depends on how it begins. So if their day initially starts out with a lot of rushing around, squabbling, and irritation, that will set the standard for the rest of their day until it mercifully draws to a close.

Yet no matter how your day begins, you always have the power to change its direction and how you respond to it. At any moment today, you could have said, "Wait! This is not the type of day I want to have. Starting now, things are going to be different. I'm going to wipe the slate clean and begin again."

You can do the same thing at night. While you may find it difficult to shake off the tensions of the day and to stop the negative tapes that play, rewind, and then replay in your mind, *you can do it*.

Before you turn out the lights tonight, say, "I had a great day! I'm proud of myself and my accomplishments. I'm happy about all the things I was able to enjoy." Ending the day with such powerful affirmations can point you in the right direction for a pleasurable evening—and the promise of a wonderful new tomorrow.

Whether I'm miles away
from home or simply feeling
miles away from others because
of my differences with them,
I can still feel that there's
purpose and meaning in my life.

The tiny points of light in the darkened sky have long been used to plot navigational courses. In fact, sailors have learned to trust the stars even more than their most sophisticated instruments. You, too, can look at the sky tonight no matter where you are and find reassurance in its light.

Perhaps you're on a business trip that has taken you away from your family or loved ones. Maybe you're on the first vacation you've taken in a long time and are feeling uncomfortable being away from work obligations and your daily routine. Perhaps you're in the military, stationed overseas, and you're feeling like a stranger in a strange land. Or maybe you're feeling alienated from others around you because of your gay lifestyle, the color of your skin, your cultural background, your level of education, or your religious beliefs.

As you take a moment to look at the sky tonight, consider that each star has meaning. Whether it's part of a major constellation or merely a pulsating, burning mass in the sky, there's a reason for that star to be there. It belongs in the sky, just as you belong in the world.

Tonight, know that you're never alone and never far from home. You're a star in the night who shares the expansive heavens with all the stars around you.

Taking a different route to or from work, spending my evenings learning something new, or doing something out of the ordinary are just a few of the ways I can make the passage of time much more interesting.

Time—and how you expe-
rience it—can be per-
plexing. When you have a
sense of expectation and
familiarity that stems from a

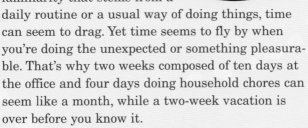

daily routine or a usual way of doing things, time
can seem to drag. Yet time seems to fly by when
you're doing the unexpected or something pleasurable. That's why two weeks composed of ten days at
the office and four days doing household chores can
seem like a month, while a two-week vacation is
over before you know it.

When your days and nights begin to blend
together in a mundane, unappealing, boring mix-
ture, then perhaps you can find ways to interrupt
the usual progression of your time and do something out of the ordinary. For example, Ronald
Graham, an internationally renowned mathemati-
cian at AT&T Bell Laboratories, has always enjoyed
the passage of time. In a 40-year time span, he has
mastered Chinese, learned to play the piano and
kept up his juggling and acrobatics, all the while
writing dozens of papers and traveling tens of thou-
sands of miles a year.

So, make time to go for a drive or a bike ride to
a place you've never been before. Take note of the
unfamiliar scenery and the novelty of your journey.
Then, when you return home, open your journal
and write down the interesting events and sights
you experienced.

Because I am always meeting new
people, I am always learning.
Tonight I trust that there's a divine
plan at work that's helping me
grow and progress as a result
of each lesson I'm given.

H ave you ever marveled at how fate has drawn you to someone? Maybe you met the person of your dreams through a very interesting turn of events. Perhaps you stopped at a store you've never been in before and discovered a childhood friend working there. Or maybe you were laid off from work, and for some reason attended a meeting in a different state and met an employer looking for someone with your qualifications.

There's a lesson to be learned from each person you meet. Your contact, however brief or extended, has occurred for a reason. Sometimes when you meet someone at a particularly meaningful time, you may feel as if you're part of a play, sharing a stage with characters you know will have an important influence on your life. Although not all the lessons you learn will make you feel wonderful—some people may treat you badly, others may leave you with pain and heartache—all will have provided you with a valuable lesson.

Tonight, trust that your life is being guided not only by the decisions you make, but also by divine forces. Rather than marveling at chance meetings and interactions that have a positive impact and questioning those that have a negative influence, accept the fact that *every* lesson you learn is meaningful.

I lure myself away from an exhausting day or the desire to do more, by creating a luxurious and inviting environment filled with scents conducive to evening relaxation. Then I breathe deeply and fall fast asleep.

The prophet Elijah—
a man of great faith—
was once reduced to
despair by a battle with
fatigue. He had overextended
himself by running nearly 120 miles from Carmel
to Berrsheba—*and* then ran an extra day's worth
through the Sinai desert! Elijah's mistake may be
similar to ones you make all the time. You think you
can put in a few extra hours of work, do the carpool-
ing for the neighborhood a couple more days, pull an
all-nighter, run an extra mile, or stay up another
hour to watch the end of a baseball game.

When you rush around in this way, you deprive
yourself of much-needed rest and relaxation. But
does that stop you? While you may drag yourself
through the next day speaking the same words as
Elijah—"It is enough!"—you may push yourself once
again the next day!

When you find yourself revved up to "go an
extra mile" this evening, soothe your restless mind
and body by preparing an aromatic bed for yourself.
Before crawling under the covers, take a warm bath
in a scented oil, lightly dab your favorite cologne on
your pulse points or pillowcase, or burn incense or
a fragrant candle in your bedroom. "Often simply
inhaling a pleasant aroma," says Susan Knaski, an
environmental psychologist, "can trigger a change in
mood and have a soothing effect."

WEEK
26

Higher Power, help me find the
strength to press onward and
upward in my quest for the truth.
Let me find my ideals and learn
to live by them. I experience great
rewards as a result.

It has been said that the truth will set you free. But what is truth? Truth is not simply being honest with yourself and others. Truth also involves the ideals you'd like to live by. To find your truth, you need to set off on an individual journey.

In many Eastern countries, people believe that truth is found after scaling a high mountain peak and consulting with a wise sage. In a way, that's what you need to do to find your truth. You need to set off on a challenging journey that will bring you closer to your Higher Power. Yet you don't have to reach the top of some majestic peak, walk the Appalachian Trail, or run a marathon in order to find your spiritual source. Rather, you can realize the truth that you find on your life's path. As you use this knowledge, your journey can become easier and less painful.

No matter how positive or negative today was, you've progressed in your search for truth. Even if you didn't move forward as far as you would have liked, you still have tomorrow. Your search for truth is an ongoing quest.

Tonight I create a list of the
positive things I can do to help
me relax when I'm restless. I keep
the list by my bed so I have it on
hand during the times I'm
troubled by insomnia.

There's nothing better than maintaining a good attitude when you're going through trying times. But when you're in the midst of a difficult situation, such as another night of insomnia, and you're stuck counting sheep, drinking warm milk, or listening to a meditation tape, you may find it difficult to see anything positive.

No matter how troubled you may feel, you can choose which pair of "attitude glasses" you'll wear. If you wear dark glasses, everything around you will appear dismal. But if you put on a pair of rose-tinted glasses, things can appear brighter. So you can either wallow in your suffering, or you can change your outlook.

Tonight you can moan, "Not another sleepless night," as you toss and turn in your darkened bedroom or watch the numbers change on your digital clock. Or you can proclaim, "Another sleepless night! What fun and exciting thing can I do to pass the time?" You may find that by taking your mind off of your inability to sleep, you can begin to relax so you can get to sleep!

The moon reminds me that
my emotions are part of me, too.
Tonight, when I express my
feelings, I remember that
I'm nourishing the soul
of my inner moon.

The moon rules the oceans. As times ebb and flow under its influence, the moon shows its presence and power. The moon is a symbol for the intuitive self; it is purported to hold court over emotions. The moon signifies abundance; the harvest moon signals a time for relaxation after the summer's labor and a time for giving thanks for a bountiful harvest. The moon is a cyclical, evolving presence; every month it moves from full and bright to black and dark.

The moon is your constant nighttime companion. Even when it isn't visible to the naked eye, its presence can still be felt. It can sway your emotions and affect your mental health, your moods, your relationships, and your energy. As a result, the moon can serve as a reminder of your connection to all things as well as your relationship to yourself.

Zen Buddhists have said that ". . . a finger is needed to point to the moon, but that we should not trouble ourselves with the finger once the moon is recognized." Tonight, take time to look at the moon. Notice its color, size, and position in the night sky. *Feel* the moon—allow its energy to fill your heart. Then sleep peacefully tonight, knowing that the moon is watching over you.

Just because I feel like I'm going nowhere doesn't mean I don't know where to go. Sometimes the smartest move I can make is no move at all. In time, I know I'll be on my true path once again.

WEEK
30

Long ago, before the advent of radar systems, navigators and explorers found it impossible to proceed on cloudy nights. Without the moon and stars to guide them, they lost the light by which they could safely see, so they had to remain where they were until morning or until the next clear night could guide them. In effect, they became powerless and had to accept their inability to progress under such conditions.

Tonight may seem like a cloudy night to you. You may feel lost or directionless. You may feel as if you're stuck in the same emotional space. You may feel powerless, unable to control circumstances that are out of your power. You may have even reached out desperately to friends, loved ones—even your Higher Power—but found no support, advice, or answers that could help you move ahead.

At a time like this, acceptance is your only answer. Just because you can't see your way clearly out of your difficulty or receive guidance to help you move on doesn't mean you'll be stuck in this uncomfortable space forever. You will move ahead, but not right now. Accept that you need to stay where you are and wait. Soon the clouds will roll away so that the moon and stars can guide you.

Tonight I pay attention
to the natural wonders
of the world. By taking
time and opening my senses,
I notice a whole new
world around me.

How often do you take time to notice the wonders of the natural world—the rainbow after a rainstorm, the birds frolicking around your bird feeder, or the silvery brilliance of a full moon? How often do you go out of your way to discover a new path through the woods or a less-traveled route to work? How often do you make time in your schedule to quietly connect with nature in some small way—by getting up early to sit in a city park and watch the sunrise slowly awaken the city, or by peering up at a star-filled night sky?

The mad rush of living—the crush of places to go, people to see, and things to do—can make you forget that there's a natural world around you that's teeming with wonders. But these wonders won't come to you; you have to take time to notice *them*.

Decide tonight that no matter how busy you are tomorrow, you're going to slow down your pace and notice the joys of nature. Pack a bag lunch so you can eat outside and feel the sun on your face. Or schedule a walk in the early evening that will take you to a place you've never been before. By becoming more aware of the world around you, you can feel more alive!

My daily activities can be my mandala. Tonight I'll stop looking for relaxation in spectacular events and concentrate, instead, on the peace that comes from the usual and the mundane.

A mandala is a painting that's often used during meditation. The brightly colored, complex image is used to increase concentration during meditation so that the meditator can become completely absorbed in it. By focusing the mind on the outer perimeter of the picture and then slowly working inwards, the meditator gradually stops paying attention to the outside world and becomes inwardly focused. When the meditator has reached the center of the mandala, that's when the meditative mind is supposedly its most open and focused.

Each day can be viewed as a mandala that can prepare you for an evening of inner peace and relaxation. By performing simple rituals each day—taking a walk or going for a run, eating meals around the same time, performing routine tasks at work or at home, or reading a little—you can still your mind.

Tonight, change the way you look at the mundane routines you perform in your life. Rather than feeling resentment about them, revel in them. They can help keep your concentration focused in soothing, positive ways.

Tonight I savor the pleasure of my own company. I think my own thoughts, curl up with a good book, or relax in a hot tub.

It's a rare person indeed who never feels lonely at night. Even when you're surrounded by friends, family, roommates, or are in the company of an intimate partner, you can still feel lonely. You may question, "What's wrong with me? I'm not alone. I have others with me." What you may not realize is that having people around sometimes puts you in touch with just how out of touch you are with yourself. Until you're happy being with yourself, it may be hard to feel content with others.

How do you create happiness in your solitude? You accept that no matter how close you are to another person or other people, you are essentially alone. You have to live within your own skin and be your own separate person. To do so takes practice. For example, instead of reaching for the telephone when you're lonely, you can listen to your favorite music. Or, you can use your alone time to give yourself a manicure, massage your feet with an aromatic oil, or create different outfits from the clothes in your closet. Connecting with yourself, rather than relying on connecting to others, is the best way to develop enriching experiences in your solitude.

Tonight, pay attention to your feelings of loneliness. Then be there for yourself. Learn that loneliness doesn't have to be bitter, and solitude doesn't have to be frightening.

Tonight I am a Spiritual Warrior.
I take action in my life, but remain
flexible and open to the will of the
universe and my Higher Power.

There's a story of a religious teacher whose daily sermons were wonderful and inspiring, and he often spent hours preparing them. He thought that someday he might compile them into a book and seek a publisher or even appear on his own television show. With these outcomes in the back of his mind, he was about to begin his sermon when a little bird came and sat on the windowsill. It began to sing with a full heart. Then it stopped and flew away. The teacher thought for a moment, folded the pages of his prepared sermon, and announced, "The sermon for this morning is over."

When you're attached to results or when you try to force things to go your way, then your sights may be set on satisfying your financial, intellectual, or emotional needs. But while many things can be sought after, worked hard for, or struggled over, some things simply exist—and exist perfectly.

Tonight, accept that a more spiritual outcome to your efforts can be equally rewarding. Release your expectations, keep an open mind to new possibilities, and enjoy connecting with the energies of a Higher Power.

Tonight I remember that
my Higher Power hears me,
no matter how I choose
to pray. Whether I spend
several minutes talking aloud
about my day or a few
moments in silence, my
Higher Power listens.

How do you learn to pray? What do you ask for? What do you say? Do you get down on your knees, bow your head, or lift your face to the heavens?

Sometimes, in trying to answer such questions, you may forget the purpose of prayer. You may feel inhibited or self-conscious about praying to an unseen presence. You may think that your prayers don't measure up to the eloquence of the sentiments expressed by a moving preacher or inspirational literature.

Tonight, if you begin to think in this way, remind yourself why you pray and what it has done for you. Although you may never describe your prayers as articulate or perfect, it's the act of praying that matters. You pray as an expression of your gratitude as well as your suffering, of your helplessness as well as your purposefulness, of your fears and doubts as well as your trust and faith, of your powerlessness as well as your strength. As Hannah More says, "Prayer is not eloquence, but earnestness; not definition of hopelessness, but the feeling of it; not figures of speech, but earnestness of soul." What's most important is making the effort to pray.

I work out the solution to any
problem tonight by reaching out
to others or using proven tools
to help channel my objectivity.
Tonight I trust that I'm capable
of soothing my troubled mind.

You may have often heard the phrase, "Things will look better in the morning." In the light of day, when you're caught up in the hustle and bustle of daily routines, the problems that troubled you the night before may recede from the shores of your mind. Upon reflection on your sleepless, restless night, you may think, *I don't know why I was so upset last night.*

But then, as the hours slowly move from day into evening and then night—and the shadows lengthen and the stream of life gradually stills—your problems may once again arise in your mind. Like specters ready to materialize at your bedroom door, they may return to haunt you.

Perhaps you trust the day more because of its light and natural rhythm. At night, the darkness obscures your vision, nature decelerates its movement, and people seem to be locked into their own rhythms. Yet you can trust tonight—and every night — by depending upon the light provided by inspirational tools. Read a favorite psalm, repeat some positive self-help affirmations, listen to the soothing advice of a friend, or reread a familiar story. Tonight can feel peaceful and trouble free when you make the effort to calm your anxious mind.

Tonight I open myself to
a mystical, magical,
or psychic moment.
I am not bound by
traditional beliefs or
the accepted "realities"
of the world.

WEEK **37**

Have you ever had a mystical, spiritual, or psychic experience? Maybe you dreamed of an event that actually came true. Perhaps you "saw" the right number to play in a lottery that resulted in financial gain. Maybe you heard the voice of a deceased loved one, who gave you encouragement, guidance, or warning. Or perhaps you were able to make it through a particularly trying time because you "knew" your Higher Power was watching over you.

Such experiences may frighten or excite you. To be able to commune in some small way with another dimension or a supernatural world can be unearthly. To be able to use your "sixth sense" can challenge your belief in the three-fold connection between mind, body, and spirit. To foresee events or to feel a protective presence may expand the boundaries of your existence. Feeling like you're more in touch with your destiny may make you feel empowered to make changes in your life.

But what do you do when you have such feelings? How do you handle the powerful impact they can have on you and your life? Tonight, don't be afraid to encourage such mystical occurrences. Use them to help you grow in ways that other experiences do not.

Sometimes I may feel like a sapling—weak, young, and unformed; other times I may feel like old wood—tired, achy, and finished with my growth. Tonight I picture the tree I'd like to be and truly feel the essence of its strength and power.

If you were a tree, what kind would you be? Perhaps you'd like to be a maple that would blossom for three seasons and then provide sweet syrup for the winter months. Maybe you'd like to be a majestic oak that would someday be cut down and used to create a beautiful piece of furniture. Perhaps you'd like to be an apple tree that would provide food and fragrance for all to enjoy year-round. Or maybe you'd like to be an evergreen that would remain forever green, wearing a nest of robins in the spring, a garland of dead leaves from surrounding trees in the fall, and a blanket of snow in the winter.

Trees may remind you of some of the people in your life whom you admire. There may be those who stand tall, never letting the difficulties of life bend them over. There may be those who radiate power and majesty as they take incredible risks or make wonderful changes in their lives. Or there may be others who remain green throughout the year, radiating a positive outlook and bountiful energy that keeps them growing strong day after day.

Tonight, consider that while you're part of a forest of "trees" that surrounds you, you're also your own unique individual tree. Which tree will you be?

Tonight my life is filled
with safety, security,
and harmony. I face
my fears of the unknown
so I can make changes
for the better.

There comes a time in
every horror movie when you
know that something terrible is going to happen.
You can feel the tension mount as your heart starts
pounding, and you may want to scream at the actors
to alert them of the impending danger.
But you can't, because it's only a film.

You may feel that same type of fear whenever
you see daylight fade and darkness approach. As
the days grow shorter and the nights grow longer,
you may feel as if you're back in the movie theater
experiencing the same sense of impending doom. Yet
life isn't a horror movie where danger lurks around
every corner and horrible things are out to get you.
So what are you afraid of? In reality, the fears you
have may spring from the shadows of the unknown.

Tonight, reflect on the words of a spiritual advi-
sor who once said: "Getting rid of fear is not easy.
When faced with a change, I may slip back to my
fear like the birds huddled on the wire. But more
often, I will welcome change like the geese do, with
gratefulness for the sign from God that it is time to
go in a new direction."

I work through my risk-taking
fears by asking, "What's the
worst possible thing that could
happen if I do this?" I take
chances and find that I grow
as a person as a result.

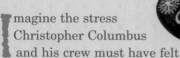

Imagine the stress Christopher Columbus and his crew must have felt as they set sail from the safe shores of their homeland, knowing that they might drop off the edge of the world and never return. But that didn't stop them from embarking on their risky voyage.

Risk-taking means attempting something new or different without the comfort of knowing what the outcome will be. Sometimes you can take a risk and achieve positive results—for instance, you may ask your boss for a raise and get it. Or you can take a risk and feel that you've struck out—for example, you may be turned down when you ask someone out on a date.

But whatever the outcome, it's important to take the risk. Being ready to take a chance doesn't mean you won't feel apprehensive. Fear is a natural reaction to the unknown. But fearing and *still taking the risk* is what risk-taking is all about. That's why the best risk-takers are the people who ask, "What do I have to lose?" They have the attitude that even if they don't succeed, like Columbus they're at least willing to try.

From now on, instead of thinking about a risk you'd like to take and what you might lose in the process, think about all you have to gain!

I make a wish upon the first star I see tonight. I receive the special gifts of newness that can greet me each dusk and dawn of my life.

The first star in the
evening sky shines
with a special brilliance
because it's the first. This
star can be seen as an impor-
tant symbol of change in the day—evening is rapid-
ly turning into night, the fall of the night curtain is
signaling the closure to the day, and the day's per-
formance is over, never again to be repeated.

The first of anything can be a symbol of something equally significant. Your first love, your first
car, your child's first words or tiny steps, your first
day of graduate school, your first job, or your
first home are all profound signals of change. Each
unique, never-to-be-repeated event becomes the
first—and most special—moment. Even though
it may be the first in a series of other loves, other
cars, another child's growth, other degrees attained,
other jobs, or other homes, the first usually has the
greatest impact on your life. For the first not only
touches you with its newness, but also signals a
time of great excitement, adventure, discovery, and
change.

Tonight, remember that when you can treat
each new day, each new person, each new experience, each new goal you set, and each new change
you make as though it were the first, your life can
be touched by excitement every day.

Tonight I view my past as
a valuable asset, my future
as a glorious new beginning,
and this moment as a time
of peace and relaxation. I rest
assured tonight, knowing
I have nothing to fear.

There's a parable about a group of congregants who were asked by their pastor to share what they

often prayed for. One who had just lost her job said secure work. Another who had medical problems said health. And another who had been raised in poverty said financial security.

But one congregant shook his head at the responses. When it was his turn, he said, "I don't pray to escape the things that frighten me. Instead, I pray for the ability to trust that no matter what happens to me each day, it is the *right* thing."

It has been said that there are two voices you can listen to. One is the voice of fear, and the other is the voice of confidence. The voice of fear is high-pitched and frantic; it whines and warns and whispers messages designed to scare you. But the voice of confidence sounds soft and soothing; it tells you not to worry, assures you that all is well, and sometimes grows silent so you can listen to your Higher Power.

Tonight, still your voice of fear, and let your voice of confidence grow louder. Pray for the wisdom to be able to live each moment to the fullest. A reassuring prayer is: "No matter what happens in the time between sunset and sunrise, I will never be surrounded by darkness."

By identifying some of the ways I can sleep better, I can improve my pre-sleep activities and behaviors. After a more restful night, the next day can be easier to get through.

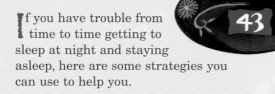

WEEK 43

If you have trouble from time to time getting to sleep at night and staying asleep, here are some strategies you can use to help you.

- *Skip a nightcap.* People who have had several drinks before bedtime often sleep very deeply during the first part of the night, but after the alcohol has been metabolized into their systems, they sleep poorly the rest of the night. So it's a good idea to limit evening alcohol consumption to one drink, at least two hours before turning in.

- *Avoid stimulants.* Coffee, tea, and chocolate aren't the only sources of caffeine. Many sodas and diet drinks contain caffeine, as do some diet pills, over-the-counter decongestants, and pain relievers.

- *Use sleeping pills sparingly.* At first, most sleeping pills may help you sleep, but after a while they can lose their effectiveness or become addictive.

- *Be in touch with your stomach.* Don't go to bed hungry or shortly after eating a heavy meal—both situations will interfere with your sleep. Also, if any food has a tendency to irritate your stomach, avoid it in the evening. You can add spice to your life—but not to your sleep!

Whenever I feel that stress
is moving me away from
my center, I do my standing,
centering meditation. I become
as firmly rooted as a tree as
I stand my ground.

Have you ever seen the ocean in a storm? The water is in constant, frightening motion, capable of sinking boats, eroding shorelines, and sweeping away entire homes. Yet below the churning surface is a stillness that enables the tiniest fish to dart gently to and fro.

Within you is a similar "center"—a part of you that's capable of being calm and still in the most nerve-wracking and restless moments. Being centered is like being a tree in a storm: while wind, rain, and lightning may affect you on the outside, your roots hold you fast and firm.

How long has it been since you felt the sensation of having your feet "planted" firmly on the ground? Aikido masters who teach their students to maintain their centers claim that it can generate incredible personal force that enables one to withstand the power of many. To gain your center at any time, stand with your feet about a foot apart. Keep your spine straight. Bend your knees slightly. Hold your hands in front of you with your elbows bent, slightly above waist level. Now inhale deeply. Imagine the energy rising up through your feet. Then exhale, feeling the energy flow out through your hands. Repeat three times, continuing to center and strengthen yourself.

Tonight I visualize that my mind is as still as the surface of a tiny pond on a sunny, windless summer day. There's nothing to disturb the surface of the water; there's nothing to disturb the inner workings of my mind.

Meditation is the process of emptying your mind of stressful thoughts so you can experience physical relaxation and inner peace. It's a way to open yourself up to communicate not only with your inner self, but also with a spiritual guide.

How do you meditate? There are no hard-and-fast rules. Some people sit in a quiet, candlelit room with their eyes closed; some listen to soothing music, recorded nature sounds, or a guided meditation tape; some chant one word; and others use running, cross-country skiing, or walking as part of their meditative exercise.

To begin meditating, select a time and place where you won't be interrupted; in that way, you become "conditioned" to calm and still your mind at that space and time. When stressful thoughts occur, simply let them float through your consciousness. Don't pay close attention to them; let them drift gently in and out of your mind. Keep your breathing steady, your body relaxed, and your thoughts stilled. You'll feel a sense of peace wash over you, and you'll be able to listen to any messages you receive from your Higher Power.

Tonight I trust the guiding voice within me so I can have faith that all things change, all wounds heal, and everything is eased through the passage of time.

Have you ever heard the story of the man who thought that God had deserted him during a most troubling time because he only saw one set of footprints along the difficult path he had just walked? When he asked God why He wasn't with him when he needed Him most, God told him that he had only seen one set of footprints because He had been carrying him.

Whether you realize it or not, the seeds of God—your faith, belief, and trust in being able to make it through troubling times—are always with you. All it takes is for you to plant them, tend to them, and let them grow.

The bird that sings before the sun has risen has planted seeds of God because it trusts that the sky will soon lighten, the sun will rise, and the world will come alive. It's when the bird doesn't sing that it loses its God seeds—and its faith.

To plant your seeds of God, keep in mind tonight that things *will* get better. There isn't a problem that can't be solved, a teardrop that won't be dried by a smile, and a weary soul who won't be energized again. Tend to your God seeds—nurture them through your prayers and meditation—so you can strengthen the faith you need to get you through the trying times.

My dreams are my
gentle emotional guides.
The more I understand
them, the better I can deal
with various emotions and
situations in my waking life.

Dreams are the messages you send yourself about the people, places, and things in your daily life for which you may have strong, often unexpressed feelings. When certain situations in your life affect you in some way, you may numb yourself so you don't feel the pain, fear, hurt, anger, tension, or sadness that such things evoke. During your waking hours, your numbing may be quite successful. But while you're sleeping, your dreams "know" these feelings and sometimes resurrect them so you have to confront them.

In your dreams, there may be scenes from the day's events that made you feel anxious or tense. You may view a collage of images that convey your fears. Or, you may get to reexperience wonderful feelings you shared with someone you loved—and lost.

Although your dreams may sometimes turn into frightening nightmares, it's important to recognize that they're simply outlets for emotions that you are not consciously expressing. Tonight, when a dream rouses you from your sleep or touches you in some way, remember that if you're honest with yourself, you can probably figure out the dream's true significance. By developing this understanding, you can then learn what feelings you need to express in your waking moments.

Everyone is a lamplighter from time to time, both for themselves and for others. I seek out a lamplighter to guide me through my darkness, or I reach out to light the path of a fellow traveler.

Before electricity was installed, city dwellers were dependent upon lamplighters to light the gas lamps before dark so they could walk at night in safety. Without light, the streets were dark and ominous— almost impassable.

Do you sometimes feel as though you're floundering about in the dark, wishing you had a lamplighter to illuminate your path? Maybe you were dependent upon someone who lit your way for a while, but then left. Perhaps you're blindly going from job interview to job interview or scanning the Help Wanted section every day in the hopes of finding a dim prospect. Maybe you feel that you're in the dark after moving to a new neighborhood or relocating to a different part of the country, far away from friends, loved ones, and familiar surroundings. Or perhaps you feel like you're in a black hole as you fall deeper into an unhealthy addiction.

Your lamplighter doesn't have to be a new lover, a new job, new friends, or a recovery process. It can simply be someone who has traveled the same darkened road you're traveling now. Reach out to a lamplighter who can help light your way by sharing some of his or her strength, hope, and experience. Until you can carry your own light, it's okay to walk under the protective safety provided by this helpful individual.

I have no idea now what's
in store for tomorrow.
Rather than try to anticipate
what will happen, I rest assured
that I will wake up feeling
refreshed and renewed.

WEEK 49

Do you always see each day as a new beginning—one that's fresh and clean and full of possibilities for the future—or do you sometimes start the day by looking back at the previous one and thinking about all the things you could have or should have done differently?

Beginning a new day with thoughts about a day gone by is like writing on a chalkboard that hasn't been washed since the start of the school year. Your new message is going to be hard to distinguish among all the other faded messages on the dusty surface. Chalky, ghostly images of minutes, hours, and days gone by make it hard to focus on the activities of the present time or to look ahead to see your future—whether that future is one minute or one year from now.

The best way to start tomorrow is to treat tonight like it's a clean slate. Tell yourself, "There's nothing I can do right now that will change the course of the day gone by." Then feel yourself being in the present—comforted in your bed, ready to have a good night's sleep, and feeling happily expectant about the day to come.

I live in the solution,
not the problem. I turn
the mundane into the
miraculous by perceiving
my everyday tasks
in a new light.

Are there routines you perform night after night that have become so tedious that they make you tense to even think about them? "I'm so tired of this!" you might scream as you pick up your children's toys, wonder what to make for dinner yet again, or sit in bed with office paperwork scattered around you.

While some situations at night will always stay the same—for example, you have to eat dinner or else you'll go to bed hungry—what you can change is the way you *perform* them. Mundane tasks can take on a new meaning when you revise your attitude toward them. Just as it can be fun to sing along with an old, familiar song, you can also make some of the routine tasks in your life more pleasurable.

Instead of feeling frustrated by scattered toys, for instance, you can make up a game you play with your child as you return toys to the box—green toys first, blue toys next, and so on. You can prepare and exchange a "mystery dinner" with a co-worker or neighbor. Or, you can listen to your favorite classical tape while you make your way through a pile of routine paperwork. Sometimes just a simple change can make your evening less routine—and much more pleasant!

Tonight I remember
that I truly experience
the full joy of living
when I can sit back
and appreciate what
I've accomplished.

Your goals lend direction to your life. Without them you might flounder, uncertain of who you are and where you're going. Goals can provide you with a source of confidence, motivate you, and give you something to look forward to.

However, at some point you need to sit back and simply enjoy your achievements. After all, what's the good of losing weight if you can't buy new clothes that will show your new figure off? What's the point of learning how to ski if you can't take off on a long weekend to a ski resort so you can enjoy your new skill? What fun is it to save money unless you can spend some of it on something you want?

It may be far easier to set goals than it is to take some time out to appreciate a goal's end. Goal setting and achieving can keep you so occupied and active that the process—not the goal—is what gives your life true meaning.

Tonight, remember that setting your sights on a goal's end is a way of accomplishing it. Appreciating a journey's end—as well as the journey itself—is what really matters.

Tonight I create happy
memories with my loved
ones that will last for a
lifetime. I choose to look
back with joy on all the
special moments in my life.

WEEK 52

Wouldn't it be nice if the warm glow, loving feelings, and laughter and lightness you feel with your loved ones tonight could burn like an eternal flame? Well, it can. From this moment on, no matter what circumstances occur or how much time passes, you can close your eyes and keep this joyous memory in your mind. See your loved ones gathered together in peace and harmony.

This doesn't mean that from now on, conflicts will be easier to handle or loving feelings will always predominate. What it *does* mean is that you can choose the memories that linger on and release the ones that are not as pleasant. It's your choice.

Tonight, delight in the shared laughter, relax with the ease of casual chatter, and thrill to a physical touch or embrace. Know that although the warm glow of togetherness may be extinguished from time to time, it can always be relit in the recesses of your mind.

About the Author

Amy E. Dean began her career as a bestselling author and nationally known speaker by writing books on self-help, personal healing, and motivational topics. Her first book, *Night Light,* sold over half a million copies, and today Amy's books are distributed worldwide.

With 15 books to her credit, Amy continues to explore issues that are relevant to everyday life and personal growth. Her nonfiction goes right to the heart and soul of her readers, offering inspirational and simple ways to approach life with greater interest, understanding, and commitment to personal fulfillment.

Amy is a graduate of Skidmore College and lives in Maynard, Massachusetts.

HAY HOUSE
Lifestyles Titles

Flip Books

101 Ways to Happiness,
by Louise L. Hay

*101 Ways to Health and
Healing,* by Louise L. Hay

101 Ways to Romance, by
Barbara De Angelis, Ph.D.

*101 Ways to Transform
Your Life,* by Dr. Wayne
W. Dyer

Books

A Garden of Thoughts,
by Louise L. Hay

Aromatherapy A–Z,
by Connie Higley, Alan
Higley, and Pat Leatham

Aromatherapy 101,
by Karen Downes

Colors & Numbers,
by Louise L. Hay

Constant Craving A–Z,
by Doreen Virtue, Ph.D.

Dream Journal,
by Leon Nacson

*Healing with Herbs and
Home Remedies A–Z,*
by Hanna Kroeger

*Healing with the Angels
Oracle Cards* (booklet
and card pack), by
Doreen Virtue, Ph.D.

Heal Your Body A–Z,
by Louise L. Hay

*Home Design with Feng
Shui A–Z,* by Terah
Kathryn Collins

Homeopathy A–Z,
by Dana Ullman, M.P.H.

Interpreting Dreams A–Z,
by Leon Nacson

Natural Gardening A–Z,
by Donald W. Trotter

Weddings A–Z,
by Deborah McCoy

*What Color Is Your
Personality?* by Carol
Ritberger, Ph.D.

What Is Spirit?, by Lexie
Brockway Potamkin

You Can Heal Your Life,
by Louise L. Hay . . .

and

Power Thought Cards and
Wisdom Cards, by Louise
L. Hay (affirmation cards)

All of the above titles may be ordered by calling
Hay House at the numbers on the next page.

We hope you enjoyed
this Hay House Lifestyles book.
If you would like to receive a
free catalog featuring additional
Hay House books and products, or if
you would like information about the
Hay Foundation, please contact:

Hay House, Inc.
P.O. Box 5100
Carlsbad, CA 92018-5100

(760) 431-7695 or **(800) 654-5126**
(760) 431-6948 (fax) or **(800) 650-5115 (fax)**

Please visit the Hay House
Website at: **hayhouse.com**